That's Not a Pet!

CAN I HAVE A PET ELEPHANT?

By Michou Franco

Gareth Stevens
PUBLISHING

Please visit our website, www.garethstevens.com. For a free color catalog of all our high-quality books, call toll free 1-800-542-2595 or fax 1-877-542-2596.

Library of Congress Cataloging-in-Publication Data

Names: Franco, Michou, author.
Title: Can I have a pet elephant? / Michou Franco.
Description: New York : Gareth Stevens Publishing, [2019] | Series: That's not a pet! | Includes index.
Identifiers: LCCN 2017040515| ISBN 9781538217887 (library bound) | ISBN 9781538217900 (pbk.) | ISBN 9781538217917 (6 pack)
Subjects: LCSH: Elephants–Juvenile literature. | Pets–Juvenile literature.
Classification: LCC QL737.P98 F693 2019 | DDC 599.67–dc23
LC record available at https://lccn.loc.gov/2017040515

First Edition

Published in 2019 by
Gareth Stevens Publishing
111 East 14th Street, Suite 349
New York, NY 10003

Editor: Therese Shea
Designer: Sarah Liddell

Photo credits: Cover, pp. 1, 11 Michael Potter11/Shutterstock.com; p. 5 Donovan van Staden/Shutterstock.com; p. 7 venusvi/Shutterstock.com; pp. 9, 21 Volodymyr Burdiak/Shutterstock.com; pp. 13, 24 (tusk) E. O./Shutterstock.com; pp. 15, 24 (trunk) Jill Morgan/Shutterstock.com; p. 17 Francois van Heerden/Shutterstock.com; p. 19 Johan Swanepoel/Shutterstock.com; p. 23 Thaninee Chuensomchit/Shutterstock.com.

Printed in the United States of America

CPSIA compliance information: Batch #CS18GS: For further information contact Gareth Stevens, New York, New York at 1-800-542-2595.

Contents

I want a pet.
I want an elephant!

Elephants are the largest land animals.

They live in Africa and Asia.

Elephants have big ears. Their ears cool them down!

Some have long teeth.
These are tusks.

Elephants have a long nose and lip. This is their trunk!

They drink with their trunk.

They pick up food
with their trunk.
They eat plants.

Elephants aren't good pets.
They're too big!

I'll see them at the zoo!

Words to Know

trunk

tusks

Index